What's in the Bible About Church?

What's in the Bible,
and Why Should I Care?

What's in the
Bible About
CHURCH

David L. Barnhart, Jr.

ABINGDON PRESS
NASHVILLE

WHAT'S IN THE BIBLE ABOUT CHURCH?
by David L. Barnhart, Jr.

ISBN-13: 978-0-687-65294-5

Manufactured in the United States of America

08 09 10 11 12 13 14 15 16 17—10 9 8 7 6 5 4 3 2 1

CONTENTS

ABOUT THE WRITER

David L. Barnhart, Jr. grew up in Huntsville, Alabama, where he attended Holmes Street and Trinity United Methodist churches. David attended Oglethorpe University, earned his M.Div. from Candler School of Theology, and finished his Ph.D. in Homiletics and Social Ethics at Vanderbilt University. He currently serves as associate pastor of Trinity United Methodist Church in Birmingham, Alabama, where he lives with his wife, his son, and their dog. He leads Contact, the contemporary worship service, and directs his church's mission and outreach programs. He is also a contributing writer for *FaithLink*.

David, a self-described geek, enjoys comic books, movies, and video games as much as he enjoys history, literature, and social theory. His hobbies include running and pinhole photography. He loves building collaborative ministries, mentoring individuals, and coaching ministry teams. He talks incessantly about language, pop culture, and the gospel. His mission is "to live and teach resurrected life in Jesus Christ among passionate people."

About This Bible Study Series

Have you ever wondered what the Bible is all about? What's in it? Why is it so important for Christians? Is it relevant for people in the 21st century? Should I care about what's in the Bible? Why? What difference will it make in my life? The study series *What's in the Bible, and Why Should I Care?* offers opportunities for you to explore these questions and others by opening the Bible, reading it, prayerfully reflecting on what the Bible readings say, and making connections between the readings and your daily life. The series title points to the two essential features of meaningful Bible study: reading the Bible and applying it to your life. This unique and exciting Bible study series is designed to help you accomplish this two-fold purpose.

The books in *What's in the Bible, and Why Should I Care?* are designed to help you find relevance, hope, and meaning for your life even if you have little or no experience with the Bible. You will discover ways the Bible can help you with major questions you may have about the nature of God, how God relates to us, and how we can relate to God. Such questions continue to be relevant whether you are new to church life, a long-time member of church, or a seeker who is curious and wants to know more.

Whether you read a study book from this series on your own or with others in a Bible study group, you will experience benefits. You will gain confidence in reading the Bible as you learn how to use and study it. You will find meaning and hope in the people and teachings of the Bible. More importantly, you will discover more about who God is and how God relates to you personally through the Bible.

What's in the Bible?

Obviously, we answer the question "What's in the Bible?" by reading it. As Christians, we understand that the stories of our faith come to us through this holy book. We view the Bible as the central document for all we believe and profess about God. It contains stories about those who came before us in the Christian faith, but it is more than a book of stories about them. The Bible tells us about God. It tells how a particular group of people in a particular part of the world over an extended period of time, inspired by God, understood and wrote about who God is and how God acted among them. The Bible also tells what God expected from them. Its value and meaning reach to all people across all time—past, present, and future.

Why Should I Care?

Meaningful Bible study inspires people to live their lives according to God's will and way. As you read through the stories collected in the Bible, you will see again and again a just and merciful God who creates, loves, saves, and heals. You will see that God expects people, who are created in the image of God (Genesis 1), to live their lives as just and merciful people of God. You will discover that God empowers people to live according to God's way. You will learn that in spite of our sin, of our tendency to turn away from God and God's ways, God continues to love and save us. This theme emerges from and unifies all the books that have been brought together in the Holy Bible.

Christians believe that God's work of love and salvation finds confirmation and completion through the life, ministry, death, and resurrection of Jesus Christ. We accept God's free gift of love and salvation through Jesus Christ; and out of gratitude, we commit our lives to following him and living as he taught us to live. Empowered by God's Holy Spirit, we grow in faith, service, and love toward God and neighbor. I pray that this Bible study series will help you experience God's love and power in your daily life. I pray that it will help you grow in your faith and commitment to Jesus Christ.

Pamela Dilmore

I remember walking through the Old City of Jerusalem, past the stones of buildings more than a thousand years old. On my first trip to the Holy Land, I had wanted to feel a sense of spiritual connection, to be able to say, "Here is where Jesus walked," and "There is where Jesus stood." Instead, as I stood in line at the Church of the Holy Sepulchre, the traditional site of Jesus' crucifixion and resurrection, I struggled with a sense of disappointment. I wondered at this strange feeling.

In the United States, when we want to honor an historical site, we put a fence around it and preserve it. We restore sites to their former state to freeze a moment in history; and we say, "This is the log cabin where Abe Lincoln was raised" or "George Washington slept here." We want to see it as it was.

However, for thousands of years, the way Christian pilgrims have honored a holy site is to build a church on top of it. When Helena, the emperor Constantine's mother, built the Church of the Holy Sepulchre, the builders singled out the tomb they believed had held the body of Jesus and razed the rest of the cliff face, obliterating any trace of what might have been the real tomb. They overlayed it with marble, gold tapestries, and oil paintings. It is unrecognizable.

Once I was able to pinpoint the source of my disappointment, I began to see the Holy Land differently. On a cool evening when I went walking in the Old City past soldiers, under ancient bridges, and by holy sites venerated by Jews, Muslims, and Christians, I stopped at a plaza near the excavations of the Temple Mount. Although the natural landscape and human cityscape have changed since the time of Jesus, I began to see a spiritual landscape that is just as important. The footsteps of millions of pilgrims have eroded this spiritual landscape into beautiful shapes. The collective faith of three religions and hundreds of cultures created these monuments to God and a humanity that desperately seeks God's face.

We do not possess the past in a pristine state. Just as Jesus' tomb isn't preserved under glass, the faith we receive has been handled by thousands of people before us. I think often, especially in the United States, we believe that we can "get back" to something in its natural, primitive, authentic state. We go through reformation after reformation, with people trying to travel back in time to that golden age of the early church, when there were (supposedly) no church conflicts and faith was simpler.

The truth is much more nuanced and complex. We can never receive faith that has been untouched by human hands and hearts. Even if we come face-to-face with God in a powerful religious experience, we still understand that experience with language we learned from someone else: sin and grace, guilt and forgiveness, love and glory. We need one another to teach, encourage, love, and support us in our faith journey.

One of the first things Jesus did in his ministry was surround himself with 12 disciples. Even Jesus needed friends on his faith journey! This small group of disciples would learn from him, support him, pray with him, and enable him to carry out his ministry. Of those, three were especially close to him; and he depended on them for moral support. When people claim that the church is an unfortunate accident, that Jesus was against organized religion, and that he never intended to create such an institution as the church, I remember that even Jesus needed spiritual friends.

Jesus patiently taught them even though they constantly missed the point and disappointed him. When he taught about his coming kingdom, James and John asked if they could be his vice presidents (Mark 10:35-37). When he demonstrated nonviolence by turning himself over to the police, Peter grabbed a sword and started swinging (John 18:10). Yet Jesus never abandoned them, though he may have sighed and rolled his eyes. I suspect that Jesus does the same thing today when his disciples fail to follow his example, but I also believe he celebrates whenever we get it right.

As we look at some of the ways of understanding the church and the church's role in the world, I hope you will see the church not just as a static organization or a collection of individuals, but a living organism. The church breaths, grows, and even reproduces just like any other living thing. It has a consciousness, a memory, and a hope for the future.

Christians make this radical claim that Jesus is God, that somehow God puts on flesh and walks around in the person of Jesus of Nazareth. It's a disturbing thought! God chooses to live in an imperfect body. God suffers blisters and body odor, fatigue and hunger. Yet it's just as scandalous to claim that God does it again—in the church. God uses this living organism to carry out God's mission in the world.

The church is certainly imperfect. We fight, and we stumble. We lose our way and pray for guidance. We go through seasons of decline and revival. Yet God chooses this body to carry on the ministry of reconciliation. What a pair of crazy ideas! First, God redeems the world through a man named Jesus, whose broken body was nailed to a cross. Next, God carries on Christ's work through a church whose body is likewise broken and resurrected again and again.

My hope in writing this book is that you will get a glimpse of that spiritual landscape we travel together. Many feet have walked the path we walk, and others will follow us. As we travel we understand who we are and what we do according to the words and deeds of Jesus. I hope that you, too, will seek out spiritual friends to support you in your journey.

Dave Barnhart

Chapter One

What Is the
CHURCH?

Bible Readings
John 13:34-35; 17:20-23; Acts 2:1-21, 37-47; 1 Corinthians 3:5-9;
Ephesians 4:4-7, 11-13

The Questions
The people who followed Jesus came to be known as the church. What is the
church? What does it do, and how does it work? What difference does church
make in our lives?

A Psalm

O come, let us sing to the LORD;

> let us make a joyful noise to the rock of our salvation!

Let us come into his presence with thanksgiving;

> let us make a joyful noise to him with songs of praise!

Psalm 95:1-2

A Prayer

Gracious God, inspire us with your Holy Spirit. As we share our spiritual journey with other people, draw us close as we draw closer to you. Knit us together into one so that we can worship you, teach each other, and serve together the world you have given us. Amen.

Images of Church

Pews and stained-glass windows. Vaulted ceilings and burning candles. Small whitewashed buildings with steeples and wide front steps. These are some of the visual images that the word *church* brings to mind. Others may imagine people: a robed preacher pounding a pulpit, diners at potluck suppers, choirs singing, volunteers building a house or working in a soup kitchen, people picketing or writing letters to the editor, missionaries carrying backpacks of medicine and Bibles to an exotic locale. Still others may think of abstract words and particular rituals: Methodist, Baptist, Catholic; justification and sanctification; Eucharist, baptism, doxology or creed.

What images come to mind when you hear the word church*?*

REFLECT

The Church Is a People

My five-year-old son stands on the steps in front of the congregation with his friends on Sunday morning. One child has his hands in his pockets. Another twirls her dress. Someone plays the piano, and then all the children begin singing. A few of them even sing in the same key:

The church is not a building, the church is not a steeple,
The church is not a resting place, the church is a people!

In just about every church, children's choirs sing this song; yet it's a hard concept to grasp. The church is not a building or an institution or an organization. The church is a people. Every person who follows Jesus is on a journey with everyone else, and together we are the church. The word usually translated as "church" is the Greek word *ekklesia*, which means "the called-out ones." In the ancient world of the New Testament, when someone called a town meeting, people would assemble in a public place. Those who gathered were the *ekklesia*, the ones who had been called out.

Our modern English word *church* also comes from Greek. It is actually made of two words: *kurios*, which means "Lord," and *oikos*, which means "house." Put together, they made the word *kuriakon*, or "Lord's house."[1] These two words, *ekklesia* and *kuriakon*, have caused a bit of confusion for us in English. One describes an assembly of people, and the other describes a building. We call the wood and brick building on the side of the road a church, but the real church is the people who meet there—or who may not meet in a building at all. The early church did not meet in buildings with steeples, pews, or stained glass. They met in homes and courtyards. They prayed, sang songs, read Scripture, shared personal stories, encouraged one another, and ate together. Then, as now, one of the main activities was sharing a meal.

What does it mean to you to say that the church is a people rather than a building?

Jesus' Vision for His Followers
John 13:34-35; 17:20-23

So if the church is the gathering of called-out ones, who did the calling?

What's in the Bible?
Read John 13:34-35 and 17:20-23. What stands out for you in these Scriptures? How does Jesus say the world will recognize his followers? What is Jesus asking for in this prayer? What do they say about our relationship with Jesus? What do they say about our relationship with one another?

Jesus himself called this assembly. In John 14:16, at this final meal with the disciples, he told them, "You did not choose me, but I chose you." John 13:34-35 is the beginning of a long farewell speech by Jesus to his disciples. In this Scripture, Jesus names the primary characteristic by which people will recognize his followers: love. Those who gather in the name of Jesus and who love one another in his name form the church. Jesus prayed not only for the disciples but for "all those who will believe in me." In this prayer, we see the vision of oneness in God through Christ. Every disciple, including each of us, who is called by Jesus is also called into community with other disciples. We share in the nature of Christ as we gather in his name.

How many people must gather before they fit the definition of *church*? Jesus set the limit as low as possible. In Matthew 18:20, he says, "Where two or three are gathered in my name, I am there among them." Of course, Jesus is with every disciple in an intimate way even when they are alone. However, when disciples gather, Jesus becomes present in a much more physical way.

How does Jesus' vision for those who follow him compare with your experience of church?

REFLECT

The Birth of the Church
Acts 2:1-21, 37-47

Though there were many disciples who followed Jesus, they didn't become the church until God touched them in a special way on the day of Pentecost. While they were worshiping together, God's Spirit filled them and began to work through them.

The Holy Spirit blew in like a storm wind and changed the gathering from a quiet prayer meeting into a loud spectacle. Some observers even thought these worshipers were drunk! Wind and fire were symbols of God's presence and life-giving Spirit. Genesis 1:2 says that just before God began creating the world, a "wind from God swept over the face of the waters." Genesis 2:7 says that when God made the first human being, God breathed "into his nostrils the breath of life." In Exodus 3:2, God spoke to Moses out of a flame and told him to free his people from slavery. The author of Acts wanted us to see that although God was doing a new thing with the church, it was also the same thing God had always done. When the Holy Spirit showed up at the disciples' gathering, it was as if God was creating the world again, delivering a message, and breathing life into the new church.

What comes to mind when you think of wind and fire? What do these images say to you about the power of God? What other images speak to you about God's power? When have you felt renewed and reborn, as though God were beginning a new chapter of your life?

REFLECT

Bible Facts

Pentecost was a festival that happened 50 days after Passover. It was called shavuot *in Hebrew. Originally a celebration of the harvest, it eventually became a day that people gathered to celebrate God giving the Ten Commandments to Moses.*

Acts 2:37-47 is like a photograph of a church gathering. In it we glimpse the life of the early communities of faith. Peter instructed the new community of believers, and his instructions offer a promise to all believers. Those early believers welcomed Peter's message and began to gather together. What they did as they gathered is what the church has done through the centuries and continues to do today: They followed the apostles' teaching, fellowshipped, broke bread, and prayed (verse 46).

Where do you see the activities described in Acts 2:46 at work in your church?

REFLECT

God's Field and God's Building
1 Corinthians 3:5-9

People who gather together as followers of Jesus Christ, as the church, do not always behave in loving ways. Paul addresses divisiveness in 1 Corinthians 3 and in so doing, he offers two images that define church: a field and a building.

What's in the Bible?
Read 1 Corinthians 3:5-9. What stands out for you in Paul's under-
standing of church? What is he saying about the relationship
between leaders and the church? What is he saying about the
relationship between the church and God?

The church at Corinth was in trouble. They had only been meeting together a few years; but personality conflicts, scandals, and religious politicking threatened to tear their community apart. There were those who thought they were more Christian than others because they had special religious experiences or had deeper theology or a special ability to know what real Christianity should look like. They fought and argued about who was right.

Paul and Apollos were workers in the early church. Paul summed up the conflict this way: "Each of you says, 'I belong to Paul,' or 'I belong to Apollos,' or 'I belong to Cephas,' or 'I belong to Christ' " (1 Corinthians 1:12). Party loyalty in church arguments had gotten out of hand. Against this kind of divided life, Paul painted a picture of the church as God's field. Each disciple plants or waters, and God gives the growth.

Jesus also used an image of growth to help the disciples gain a better understanding of themselves as his followers. He gathered his closest disciples in a room on the night before he died. Together, they celebrated the Passover meal. At that meal, he told them, "I am the vine, you are the branches" (John 15:5).

I attended a friend's wedding near San Francisco. The reception was held at a winery, and we sat under a trellis of grapevines. Bunches of rich, red grapes hung pendulously over our heads. Looking at them, I could imagine a vineyard owner checking them all season, hoping and praying they would receive just the right amount of rain. Too much and the grapes would burst; too little and they would be small and hard. I imagined her pruning back unnecessary suckers and tying up trailing branches to the trellis.

As we sat under those grapes that evening, with the stars shining through the leaves, surrounded by abundant life, I thought about these words of Jesus. A branch severed from the vine withers and dies, but a fruitful branch connected to the vine grows heavy with succulent grapes. In a similar way, followers of Jesus who intentionally stay connected with Jesus produce fruit in their own lives. In Jesus' image of the vine and branches and in Paul's image of the church as God's field, the church is a living, organic thing. It is not merely a social organization. It is not merely a charitable nonprofit group. The church's good works, its fruit, grows out of its deep life-giving connection to Jesus.

What does the image of God's field say to you about the church? How do the people in the church plant and water? How does the image of the church as a branch of the vine of Christ speak to you?

REFLECT

Even though the children's song says, "The church is not a building," Paul's image in First Corinthians includes the idea of the church as God's building. Peter used building language to describe the church (1 Peter 2:4-5). Peter spoke of God as a cosmic architect, building upon Jesus, the cornerstone. Paul also talked about building on the foundation, which is Jesus Christ (1 Corinthians 3:11). He asked the church at Corinth, "Do you not know that you are God's temple and that God's Spirit dwells in you?" (verse 16). Paul said that we gathered disciples are the temple. Together, we create a home for God's Spirit, which lives within us.

What does the image of God's building say to you about the church? How do you think the people in the church build?

REFLECT

One Body, One Spirit, Many Gifts
Ephesians 4:4-7, 11-13

People often lament the fact that the modern church looks little like the early church in Acts. The inspirational descriptions of the church in Acts 2:43-47 and 4:32-37 sound like utopia, a growing community of thousands, where everyone loved one another, nobody lacked for essentials, and all the Christians were of one heart and mind. Who wouldn't want to be part of such a movement? In spite of our human tendency toward conflict, the vision of church persists. It is a vision that recognizes and celebrates human differences in light of oneness in Christ.

It didn't take long before favoritism and hurt feelings began to make the disciples aware that they needed a way of organizing and dividing their labor. Even in the early days, the followers of Jesus had to deal with the practical everyday business of living. Although it isn't as inspiring to talk about organizing strategies and systems, the early church had to organize as their size increased. In Acts 6:1-6, we hear that there were those who felt neglected in the daily distribution of food. Though Luke doesn't spend a lot of time on this conflict, it's easy to imagine how painful this kind of church conflict could be. It may have started with one or two people grumbling about being overlooked and gradually grew until some people felt the church was divided into "us" and "them."

The same thing happens in many churches today. Real or perceived favoritism leads people to think in terms of "us" and "them," young and old, newcomers and old-timers, minority and majority, immigrant and native. Leaders often find that they spend too much time doing diplomacy, soothing hurt feelings, and caring for bruised egos than in casting a vision for their churches. Many pastors feel they have so many obligations to care for members that they do not have time to lead the church to do its ministry in the world.

The early church found one solution to this problem: delegating. They chose seven people to be in charge of distributing food (Acts 6:3). They divided the labor. If a group of disciples is small, it is okay to function relatively informally, with everyone pitching in whenever they see a need. As the group grows larger, it becomes necessary to organize. Just as a physical body is made up of organs and organ systems, the body of Christ also needs organization and a division of labor. Ephesians 4:11-13 celebrates the practicality of diverse gifts that make such division of labor possible. Spirit creates the oneness of the church and empowers it to recognize the different skills, gifts, and ideas of its members.

Think about the last time you participated in a group activity. Maybe it was going with friends to a picnic or a movie. Perhaps it was going on vacation or something as simple as making dinner. What were the tasks that needed to happen? Who drove or navigated? Who brought the food? Who made the phone calls or communicated with other people to pull off the event? What connections can you make between this event and the division of labor in Ephesians 4?

REFLECT

Ephesians 4:11-12 reveals that Christian leadership was obviously important in the growth and spread of the early church. Today, various churches practice all kinds of church leadership and mean different things when they say deacon, elder, priest, pastor, minister, bishop, teacher, evangelist, and lay leader. The important thing is that leaders, whether they are church members or clergy, help the rest of the body of Christ organize and carry out its ministry or, as we read in Ephesians 4:12, "equip the saints for the work of ministry, for building up the body of Christ." This ministry of church is for a purpose, a vision that gleams in verse 13. The church does this ministry so that "all of us come to the unity of the faith and of the knowledge of the Son of God, to maturity, to the measure of the full stature of Christ."

Have you ever thought of yourself as a saint? What does it mean to you to grow into "the full stature of Christ"? How might fellow saints help one another to grow into maturity?

REFLECT

Living and Growing Together

Looking at the early church in the Bible helps us learn about the church today. It reminds us that we are always growing and changing into the disciples that God created us to be. It also reminds us that the church is not static. Like a vine, we grow. Like a body, we move. Like a family, we love and support one another, celebrating every time God adds another brother or a sister or a new child in our midst. Part of the joy of being the church together is that we share a journey of faith, and our journey carries the potential of meaning and transformation through Christ for all people.

Here's Why I Care
How is the vision of church in this chapter similar or different from the way you usually think about church? Has it changed the way you think about your own role in relation to other followers of Jesus?

A Prayer

God, we thank you that we do not have to make the journey of faith alone. You give us traveling companions and guides along the way. We thank you for the awesome honor and frightening responsibility of being your body for the world. Help us live up to the task. Amen.

---

[1]From *www.etymonline.com/index.php?term=church.*

Chapter Two

THE CHURCH
Worships

Bible Readings
Exodus 3:1-6; 33:18-23; 34:28-34; 2 Samuel 6:12-19; Psalm 150;
Matthew 3:13-17; 6:1-21; 28:16-20; Luke 22:14-20; John 4:4-24;
1 Corinthians 11:23-26

The Questions
Throughout the Bible we find stories about God's people and worship. What can we learn from the Bible about worship? Why do we gather with others to worship? How do we worship? How can worship change us?

A Psalm

Make a joyful noise to the LORD, all the earth.

Worship the LORD with gladness;

come into his presence with singing.

Know that the LORD is God.

It is he that made us, and we are his;

we are his people, and the sheep of his pasture.

Enter his gates with thanksgiving,

and his courts with praise.

Give thanks to him, bless his name.

For the LORD is good;

his steadfast love endures for ever,

and his faithfulness to all generations.

Psalm 100

A Prayer

Mysterious God, all creation sings of your glory; yet we do not even know how to begin to address you. Words cannot describe or contain you. Like confetti thrown toward the sun, our language falls far short. Yet your beauty and glory moves us to gesture toward you, to give you honor and praise. Accept our songs, our dances, and our words as an offering to you. Amen.

Glimpses of Glory

Something about God's glory moves us to worship God. We are familiar with this feeling in everyday life. In her book *On Beauty and Being Just,* Elaine Scarry describes the effect beauty has on us: "Each of us has, upon suddenly seeing someone beautiful, tripped on the sidewalk, broken out in a sweat of new plumage, dropped packages (as though offering a gift or sacrifice)—all while the bus we were waiting for pulls up and pulls away."[1] We gasp at the bigness of the universe as we lie on our backs and stare at the night sky on a moonless night, the stars scattered like dust across the heavens. We get caught up in the perfect yellow-green spiral in the center of a sunflower or catch our breaths as we hold a newborn and touch her soft cheek. These tiny glimpses of glory leave us aching for more, so sometimes we can understand what it would mean to be overwhelmed by God's glory. We say things like, "I'm so happy I could burst" or "cry" or even "die." Something shines for us in such experiences.

Have you ever experienced an overwhelming sense of beauty or glory? What was it like? Where do you see God's glory? Have you experienced God's glory in worship? outside of worship? Does worship make you more aware of God's glory around you? If so, how?

REFLECT

Glory to God
Exodus 3:1-6; 33:18-23; 34:28-34

Moses had several "shining" experiences with God in Exodus that offer glimpses of what worship is all about: encounters with God.

What's in the Bible?
Read Exodus 3:1-6; 33:18-23; 34:28-34. What stands out for you in these Scriptures? How do you respond to the images of fire and light? What do they say to you about the sense of God's presence? What connections do you see between these Scriptures and worship in church?

For Moses, the encounters began with a burning bush (Exodus 3:1-6). This holy encounter led to Moses' mission to free the people from slavery in Egypt, lead them through the wilderness, and communicate God's covenant and law to them. In Exodus 33:18, Moses asks to see God's glory. Moses didn't see God's face; he saw God's back. God told Moses that the reason he wouldn't allow Moses to see his face was that "no one shall see me and live" (Exodus 33:20). When God established the covenant with the people of Israel through Moses, and after speaking with God, Moses' face shone so brightly that other people were afraid of him (Exodus 34:30). Elijah likewise had a close encounter with God; he kept his face covered while they talked (1 Kings 19:12-13). Jesus and three of his closest disciples also had an out-of-time experience with Moses and Elijah on top of a mountain (Luke 9:28-43). Just as with Moses, Jesus' face shone; and even his clothes became "dazzling white" (Luke 9:29). Something about God's presence and God's glory is contagious. People who have a close encounter with God seem to shine.

Worship isn't always this way. People sometimes say that worship bores them because they are singing the same old songs and listening to tiresome sermons. However, in those moments when we experience glory, when the goosebumps stand up along our spine, we, like Moses, get a glimpse of God. Our glimpses give us a sense of that we are called to something larger. The word *worship* comes from the same Old English root word as *worth*. Worship is the act of giving "worth," praise, and value to God.

How do you respond to the sentence "Worship is the act of giving 'worth,' praise, and value to God"? How do you see this in your church worship service?

REFLECT

20

Bible Facts

Several words in the Bible are translated as "worship." The Hebrew word is shachah, *which means to "bow down." When Moses talked with God, he worshiped in this way (Exodus 34:8). The Greek word* proskuneo *means "to bow and kiss the hand of some honored or royal person" (John 4:24). When people worshiped Jesus, they probably showed their devotion by kissing his hand. Another Hebrew word translated as "worship" is* abad, *which literally means "to serve" (Judges 2:11). In Greek, the word is* latreo. *The Bible usually uses this word to talk about priests offering sacrifices or carrying out their duties in the Temple.*

David Dances Before the Lord
2 Samuel 6:12-19

Though there are people who have objected to dancing for religious reasons, dance has been part of worship for generations. King David danced as the priests paraded the ark of God, the symbol of God's presence, into Jerusalem.

What's in the Bible?

Read 2 Samuel 6:12-19. How do you respond to David's worship in this Scripture reading? What connections do you make between this Scripture and worship in churches today?

The Bible says David "danced before the LORD with all his might" (2 Samuel 6:14), so this was no relaxed formal stepping but leaping and furious movement (2 Samuel 6:16). Miriam, Moses' sister, led the women in dancing after the Hebrews escaped Egypt (Exodus 15:20). Psalm 149:3 calls people to "praise [God's] name with dancing, / making melody to him with tambourine and lyre." Dance helps remind us that our bodies are also part of our spiritual life. We human beings bring our minds and our bodies to worship, and we can worship God with our bodies as well as our minds. We are not limited to expressing joy with smiles; we can use our arms and legs as well. We can express reverence not only by closing our eyes but by bowing or kneeling. David's wife Michal disapproved of David's actions (2 Samuel 6:16). Such responses occur today as well. Sometimes when a worshiper becomes "too emotional" or "carried away" with worship, they bump against what is considered socially acceptable.

Though we live in a culture that tends to think of religion as a personal and private matter, worship is a public act. We gather with other people and become part of a community. We join with other people to give God glory and affirm what we believe. Hebrews 10:24-25 encourages Christians to consider how to "provoke one another to love and good deeds, not neglecting to meet together, as is the habit of some, but encouraging one another." There are many different aspects of worship that engage all the senses. We see paintings or banners or stained-glass windows. We smell candles or incense. We feel the movement of our bodies or the water of baptism. We hear music or preaching. We taste the bread and wine of Communion. Each action speaks to different people in different ways. It is helpful to remember that worship takes many different forms because people experience God's presence in many different ways.

Are there times when other people's worship made you uncomfortable? What was the situation? What made you feel uncomfortable? Why?

REFLECT

David brought the ark of God into the sacred tent set aside for it. He offered "burnt offerings and offerings of well-being" to God and then blessed the people and distributed food to them (2 Samuel 6:17-19). All these actions were part of the worship celebration and gave the people the assurance that God was with them in the midst of Jerusalem.

How do you respond to the distribution of food to the people as part of the worship celebration?

REFLECT

Music and Worship
Psalm 150

David danced as an act of worship. The person who wrote Psalm 150 tells us to praise God with music.

What's in the Bible?
Read Psalm 150. What are the instruments that are mentioned? If you were to rewrite this psalm with modern instruments, what instruments would you include?

In our modern society, we are surrounded by music. Some of us use personal music players. The radio, television, and the Internet give us music on demand. It's hard to imagine that less than a hundred years ago there were only two ways to get music: You made it, or you went to where people were making it. All music was live. If you wanted to make music, you could use your voice. If you could afford it and if you had the skill, you could make music with an instrument, such as a guitar or a piano. The main places you would go to make music with other people were the fields (where you might sing while working), the pub or saloon, or the church. In our society, music has become a product we consume instead of something we make. Worship is one of the few places (outside of karaoke bars) where people still sing. Yet there is something powerful about uniting our individual voices as a group. At a concert I attended not long ago, the band stopped playing at several points during their more popular songs and the crowd continued singing the familiar lyrics. Those moments were magical. I felt a sense of kinship and love with all those strangers, part of a sea of humanity, as we sang together.

What kinds of music appeal to you? Do you sing in the car or the shower? Do you sing in public? What kinds of songs inspire you to sing along? If you were to make a soundtrack to your life, what music would be on it? What kinds of music help you worship God?

REFLECT

A Matter of the Heart
Matthew 6:1-21

In Matthew 6:1-21, a section from the Sermon on the Mount, Jesus teaches about several practices closely associated with worship: giving to those in need, prayer, and fasting.

What's in the Bible?
Read Matthew 6:1-21. How do you respond to Jesus' teachings in this Scripture? What does it say to you about worship?

Giving to Others

At first glance, almsgiving or giving to others in need, may not seem to be an act of worship. For Jesus, giving is a practice of piety, that is, a worshipful practice of justice and righteousness that benefits others and serves God. In the New Testament, the author of Hebrews says that our good deeds and sharing our resources are acts of worship (Hebrews 13:16). Giving is a matter of the heart, not a matter of show (Matthew 6:2-4).

How do you respond to the idea that giving to others is an act of worship?

REFLECT

Prayer

Prayer is perhaps the easiest and most natural kind of worship. We can pray anywhere, even in a car or a bus or while walking. Prayer is simply conversation with God. It may involve speaking with our lips, meditating silently, or listening intently for a nudge or an experience of God. Jesus warns against ostentatious displays of prayer (Matthew 6:5-7). Sincere conversation with God leaves no room for grandstanding. However, that doesn't mean we should never pray in public.

I watched a father talking with his daughter on the playground.

"Do you know how much I love you?" he asked. She grinned and held out her arms.

"This much?" she asked.

"Bigger," he replied.

"This much?" she asked, stretching them further and standing on her tiptoes.

"Even bigger," he said.

Laughing, she jumped into the air with her arms spread wide, shouting, "This much?"

He caught her in the air and yelled, "This much!" and swung her through the air while she laughed.

Watching them, I knew this was not the first time they had spoken this well-rehearsed conversation. I thought to myself how much it was like a call and response we sometimes use in worship. The leader says, "Let the people of God say amen"; and they reply, "Amen." Or the leader says, "Let us give thanks to the Lord our God"; and they say, "It is right to give our thanks and praise."

The Bible encourages us to pray with others. Praying with others might involve one person leading others in a spoken prayer. It might mean reading a prayer together or everyone speaking at once. Some people feel that prayers should not be read or recited, only spoken spontaneously. They say it feels more genuine and God-inspired. Yet Jesus himself frequently prayed in the words of the Psalms. It can be powerful to use words that generations of faithful people have used to address God. The well-known words of the Lord's Prayer in Matthew 6:9-13 have been repeated by people of faith since the beginning of the church.

Have you prayed the Lord's Prayer? What would it mean for God's will to be done on earth as it is in heaven? Do you think people think about these words when they pray them?

REFLECT

Fasting

Fasting or abstinence has been an act of worship for thousands of years. While those with health issues need to be conscientious about food, the purpose of fasting is to help people connect with their need for God. As with giving to others and prayer, Jesus' main point is to avoid fasting for show. What counts is the relationship with God. In this sense, fasting can be a helpful form of worship. It can also help us identify with the needs of those who are hungry.

How do you respond to the idea of fasting as a form of worship?

REFLECT

Money

In Matthew 6:19-21, Jesus addresses the uselessness of trusting in worldly goods. The question here is, What do we worship? (Matthew 6:21). Yet, our "treasure" also provides an opportunity for worship. Money is a measure of what we value. For this reason, money has spiritual power. Ancient people brought whatever they had produced—grain, animals, oil, or wine—as an offering to God. They brought the first fruits of their harvest. In our society, our production is generally not in the form of grain or animals, but dollars. We continue the tradition of bringing our offerings to God. Honoring God with our money is an important dimension of worship.

True Worship
John 4:4-24

In John 4:4-24, Jesus engages in an unusual conversation with a Samaritan woman about worship.

What's in the Bible?
Read John 4:4-24. What images stand out for you in this story? How do the images of water and thirst speak to you about true worship?

Jesus broke two social barriers by entering into conversation with the Samaritan woman at the well. First, Jews and Samaritans had a long history of mutual dislike and enmity. Much of their enmity involved differences in the practice of their religion. Second, it was not customary or socially acceptable for rabbis (teachers) to speak to women in public (John 4:9). However, Jesus used the opportunity to talk about living water that quenches spiritual thirst and leads to eternal life. Then the conversation moved toward a discussion about the place of worship. Samaritans traditionally worshiped in a temple on Mount Gerizim. The place of worship for the Jews was the Temple in Jerusalem. Jesus taught that the most important aspect of worship is not the place but the spirit of worship (verse 24).

What places have been helpful to you in your worship? What does it mean to you to worship in Spirit and truth?

R E F L E C T

Baptism and the Lord's Supper
Matthew 3:13-17; 28:16-20; Luke 22:14-20; 1 Corinthians 11:23-26

Christians celebrate the rituals of baptism and the Lord's Supper. Both rituals have been part of Christian worship since the beginning.

Baptism (Matthew 3:13-17; 28:16-20)
Baptism is the act of incorporating new Christians into the body of Christ in a ritual that involves the use of water by immersion, pouring, or sprinkling.

What's in the Bible?
Read Matthew 3:13-17; 28:16-20. What do these Scriptures say to you about baptism?

In Matthew 3:13-17, Jesus chose to be baptized by John in the Jordan River. In so doing he accepted his call from God and expressed his commitment to God's purposes. The reading contains God's response of love and approval for his actions. Matthew 28:16-20 is called "The Great Commission." In this Scripture, Jesus reassures the disciples that God had given him authority "in heaven and on earth" and told them to "go therefore and make disciples of all nations, baptizing them in the name of the Father and of the Son and the Holy Spirit." He also instructed them to teach others what he had taught them. Both these Scriptures illuminate the call to all who choose to follow Jesus and to live as he taught.

Christians do not live just for themselves. They are called to participate in God's will for all by reaching out to others. When Christians baptize others or remember their own baptisms, they are reminded of God's call to be the people of God through Christ. In addition, churches find meaning in baptism as a cleansing from sin and as dying and rising with Christ and living in his resurrection. All believe baptism is a way to experience God's grace. In Acts 8:36-39, Philip meets a government official from Ethiopia. He asked to be baptized in the first puddle they saw on the side of the road! The official was a eunuch, someone who would never officially be allowed into the Temple in Jerusalem. The fact that Philip baptized this outsider on the side of the road demonstrates that anyone, anywhere can become part of the family of God.

*How is baptism practiced in your local church? How does the
symbolism of the water speak to you?*

R
E
F
L
E
C
T

The Lord's Supper (Luke 22:14-20; 1 Corinthians 11:23-26)

The Lord's Supper is also called Eucharist or Communion. This act of worship involves telling the story of Jesus' last night with his disciples when they celebrated the Passover meal together.

What's in the Bible?
*Read Luke 22:14-20 and 1 Corinthians 11:23-26. What do the
Scriptures say to you about the Lord's Supper?*

In Luke 22:14-20 (see also Matthew 26:26-29 and Mark 14:22-25), Jesus calls the wine "my blood" and the bread "my body." In doing this, Jesus was reinterpreting a meal practiced by ancient Jews since the time of Moses. This meal was called Passover and reminded them of the night God set them free from slavery in Egypt (Exodus 12:24-27).

We can tell from Paul's letters that celebrating the Lord's Supper had become a ritual of the church from early on. In 1 Corinthians 11:23-26, he tells the story almost verbatim, indicating that it was language the first Christians knew by heart. We use the same language in our worship today. Paul also said that by sharing the blood and body of Christ, we become the body of Christ (1 Corinthians 10:16-17). As we celebrate the Lord's Supper, we remember what Jesus did for us through his ministry, his suffering and death, and his resurrection. We also remember that through Christ, God empowers us to give ourselves in service to God and to others.

How is the Lord's Supper practiced in your local church? How does the symbolism of the bread and the wine speak to you?

REFLECT

Worship and Life

All these biblical teachings point to the deep connection between worship and life. When Martin Luther King, Jr. gave his famous "I Have a Dream" speech in Washington, DC, he was speaking directly to American Christians in the words of a prophet, reprimanding them for giving God lip-service but not worshiping God with their lives. It certainly is possible for people to worship God on Sunday and live how they please the rest of the week. However, the Bible paints a picture of worship in which our praise of God flows into every aspect of our lives so that we worship God not only at special times with others but in our daily business of living.

Here's Why I Care

In this chapter we have explored worship and what it means to give God glory. What kind of worship speaks most to you? How do you experience glory in your worship? How can worship spill over into your daily life?

A Prayer

God of grace and God of glory, let us reflect your glory to all those around us. Thank you for giving us glimpses of your beauty. We praise you with our words. Help us praise you in deeds as well. Amen.

---

[1] From *On Beauty and Being Just*, by Elaine Scarry (Princeton University Press, 1999); page 76.

Chapter Three

THE CHURCH
Teaches

Bible Readings
Exodus 12:21-28; Deuteronomy 4:1-10; 11:18-21; Mark 4:1-20;
Acts 18:24-27; Colossians 3:12-17

The Questions
The church is a group of people called to teach others about God and about living as God's people. What does the Bible say about teaching God's way of life to others?

A Psalm

Teach me, O LORD, the way of your statutes,

and I will observe it to the end.

Give me understanding, that I may keep your law

and observe it with my whole heart.

Psalm 119:33-34

A Prayer

Jesus, our teacher and mentor, give us hearts and minds humble enough to admit what we do not know and to learn from you and one another. We know that we cannot learn as long as we believe we have all the answers. Teach us wisdom as well as knowledge. Inspire us to be like you, not only in our thoughts but in our words, and not only in our words but in our actions; in your name, we pray. Amen.

The Primary Source

The Bible has much to say about who God is and how God relates to all God has created. In its pages we learn about One who is merciful, just, and compassionate. God creates, saves, restores, and provides. God enters into relationship with us and calls those who respond to live according to God's ways of mercy, justice, and love. God's people are called to love God and to love neighbor, which is the central message of our faith; but the Bible doesn't stop here. It also calls God's people to teach these learnings and practices to others.

Many people think spiritual things don't need to be taught; we should just know God intuitively, but the Bible takes a pragmatic view of God. God is active in history, calling people and revealing God's self to them. In order to know and understand God, we must also know and understand God's history. What has God been up to in history? What kinds of things has God done, and what kinds of things have people done in response? The church teaches the Bible. We tell the stories of the Bible in worship. We refer to Scripture in our hymns, read and expound on it in sermons, study it in Bible

36

studies and Sunday schools, and encourage people to read it on their own. When we confront a problem in the church or an issue in society, we look to the Bible to see how the stories it tells and the ideas it presents relate to our own situation.

Because my name is David, I always looked forward to hearing the story of David and Goliath when I was a child. I enjoyed hearing my name read from the pulpit or spoken in Sunday school. I also enjoyed it because in the story David is a young boy who defeats a giant warrior. I liked to imagine that I, too, could wield a slingshot and bring down a powerful bully. Then I would be cheered and celebrated as a hero. The Bible invites us all to imagine ourselves in the pages of the story. The Bible also invites us to stretch our imaginations a bit further and imagine not only ourselves but our community in the Bible story. The earliest readers of the Bible remembered constantly that God freed their ancestors from slavery to the Egyptians. They were reminded that they had once been aliens in a foreign land. The Bible also reminded them that God had stuck by them through thick and thin.

Second Timothy 3:16-17 says, "All Scripture is inspired by God and is useful for teaching, for reproof, for correction, and for training in righteousness, so that everyone who belongs to God may be proficient, equipped for every good work." The assertion that Scripture is inspired and useful continues in the church today. This chapter offers the opportunity to explore several key Scriptures from the Old and New Testaments that inform what the church is called to teach about God's way of life.

Which Bible stories especially appeal to you? Why? How do you understand the idea that the Bible is inspired by God and useful for teaching and equipping people for good work?

REFLECT

Remember What God Did for Us
Exodus 12:21-28

The church teaches people about God. This means that there are things about God that need to be taught. The church, or someone in the church, knows those things and can teach them. We see this concern for teaching early in the history of God's people in Exodus 12:21-28.

What's in the Bible?
Read Exodus 12:21-28. What challenges you or especially strikes you about this Scripture? What does it tell you about God? What methods are described to help the people remember how God saved them? How do you respond to these methods for remembering?

Exodus 12:21-28 tells about the traditions associated with the observance of Passover. It emphasizes the importance of remembering how God delivered the people of Israel from slavery in Egypt. It tells the people to continue observing Passover so they will remember how the destroyer "passed over" their houses when the first-born of all the Egyptians were killed. After this final plague, Moses was able to lead the people out of slavery in Egypt. Exodus 12:24 focuses on the importance of remembering God's actions and of teaching the observance to their children in order that they will also remember.

The church continues to teach the biblical stories about God and God's people in such settings as Sunday school, worship, vacation Bible school, and other Christian education groups. Exodus 12 reveals that it was important for the Israelites to remember and to teach their children about God's actions to save them. Such remembering and teaching continues to be important in the contemporary church.

38

Walk the Talk, Heart and Soul
Deuteronomy 4:1-10; 11:18-21

The Scripture readings in Deuteronomy point to the importance of remembering, teaching, and living God's way of life.

Deuteronomy 4:1-10

When God chose the people of Israel to be God's covenant people, God had certain things in mind. Choosing them was part of a plan to capture the attention of the world. Other nations would look at them with awe, and they would become role models for God's way of life.

What's in the Bible?
Read Deuteronomy 4:1-10. How do you respond to the way God is portrayed here? Who have been role models for you in your life? How does an ideal community look and act?

39

The idea of teaching by example presupposes a certain way of living and acting. God's people are expected to live according to God's way. In Deuteronomy 4:1, 2, God says other people would look at Israel and say, "Surely this great nation is a wise and discerning people! For what other nation has a god so near to it as the LORD our God?" (Deuteronomy 4:6-7).

I recently spoke with a rabbi who told me that "just because Jews have a special covenant relationship with God doesn't mean other people don't have a relationship with God. Our role is to be an example, so that the world will know God better." Christians also carry out this mission. Jesus, an observant Jew who was deeply faithful to the traditions he received from those who came before him, called his followers "the salt of the earth (Matthew 5:13), "the light of the world," and "a city built on a hill" (Matthew 5:14). Part of the role of being a disciple, a learner and follower of Jesus, is to be an example for the world (Matthew 5:16).

Deuteronomy 4:1-10 reveals what we in the church often call "walking the talk." Not only are we called to teach, we are called to practice what we teach. We learn the principles of living a good life from the teachings given to us in the Bible, and we learn from other people by watching how they live those principles. As teachers and as learners of our Christian faith, our goal is to be transformed and to transform others. We learn about God, learn what is in the Bible, and learn the disciplines of living a Christian life. We teach in order to transform individuals, communities, and the world.

What does the phrase walk the talk *suggest to you? How do you connect this phrase to Deuteronomy 4:1-10?*

REFLECT

Deuteronomy 11:18-21

In order to walk the talk and to teach their children and others about God's way of life, God's people must continue to remember the instructions or commandments for living God's way.

What's in the Bible?
Read Deuteronomy 11:18-21. How do you respond to this reading? What images particularly strike you? Why? What does putting God's words in your heart and soul suggest to you?

In Deuteronomy 11:18-21, God gives the Israelites instructions for keeping God's words before them all the time. Teach the children. Talk about the laws at home and away from home. Remember them when you wake up and when you go to bed. This kind of disciplined learning was meant not only to transform individuals but to create a community of learners and teachers who had an intimate, personal relationship with God. As in Exodus 12 and in Deuteronomy 4, we see the importance of teaching the children about God's way of life. Again, remembering, learning, and teaching go together. The lifestyle God describes was not only for their personal or community enjoyment; it was meant to transform the world.

There are three main ways the church teaches God's way of life: worship, study, and service. We could say that worship transforms our hearts, study transforms our minds, and service transforms our lives. Of course, all of these overlap; but the process of teaching and learning transforms the whole person. In public worship or private devotion, when we hear Scripture read and proclaimed, when we sing songs and pray in community or alone, we are learning and being transformed in our hearts. When we study the Bible and discuss it with others, we transform our minds through dialogue and grow in our knowledge of Scripture. When we serve, we experience interpersonal learning. We meet God in our neighbors and learn by putting our faith into action.

We allow God to shape us by integrating these teachings into our daily business of living. As followers of God's way of life, we learn and are transformed so that we may transform the world.

What are your repeated daily rituals of waking up, eating, and getting ready for bed? What tools do you use to remember something important? How can you use your daily rituals to remember and practice God's way of life?

REFLECT

Sowing Seeds
Mark 4:1-20

Mark 4:1-20 shows Jesus in his role as teacher. He tells a story about seeds and soils that reveals much about teaching, learning, and living God's way.

What's in the Bible?
Read Mark 4:1-20. How do you respond to this story that Jesus uses to teach? What does it say to you about teaching God's way of life? What does it say to you about learning God's way of life?

One of the main ways Jesus taught was by telling stories. The stories he told were called parables. Storytelling allowed Jesus to make a point in a much more poignant way than simply stating facts. We tell parables all the time. Often these stories have a clear lesson or moral. One example of a commonly known parable that many of us learn in childhood is the story of the tortoise and the hare. The slow-going tortoise wins a race against the hare that sprints but stops to nap. Many of the jokes we tell are actually parables, and sometimes their lessons or morals are a bit more vague. We tell jokes about arrogant people getting their comeuppance or foolish people saying or doing something surprisingly profound. Jesus used parables in the same way. They amuse, surprise, shock, or puzzle us while they illustrate Jesus' teachings.

Bible Facts
The word parable *comes from two Greek words:* para, *meaning "around," and* bole, *meaning "to throw." It is related to the word* parabola, *the arc made when a ball is thrown through the air. A parable is a story that goes around a point instead of just coming out and saying it.*

BIBLE FACTS

The story about sowing seeds speaks loudly to the necessity of teaching God's way in spite of how the words might be received by those who listen. Listeners may be rocky soil, thin soil, weedy soil, or good soil; and the seeds of God's word fall into each kind. When the church is faithful and teaches God's way as it is called to do, the expectation is that people will experience transformation in their lives. Such transformation may or may not happen, yet the church continues to sow the seeds of God's word. Small as the seeds may be, some will fall on good soil. The church is called to teach and to trust God to transform people's lives.

Priscilla and Aquila Teach Apollos
Acts 18:24-27

In Acts 18:24-27, we see the importance of mutual support as we teach and learn together what it means to be Christian.

What's in the Bible
Read Acts 18:24-27. Have you ever heard teaching that was articulately and eloquently wrong? How did you feel for the person speaking or teaching? How do you respond to the actions of Priscilla and Aquila in this story?

Priscilla and Aquila recognized the intelligence and enthusiasm of Apollos when they heard him teach, but something was not right with what they heard. Rather than discount him, they "took him aside and explained the Way of God to him more accurately" (Acts 18:26). Then the believers in their community encouraged Apollos and wrote letters to the disciples on his behalf. As a result, Apollos continued an effective ministry. The story demonstrates how the church functions to teach and support people as they grow in faith.

I once sat in a waiting room with a family while the grandmother slowly died in intensive care. We prayed together for God's healing presence to be with her to ease her pain. When we finished, a young woman who had over-heard announced that she no longer prayed for healing. She said that a friend of hers had prayed for healing for her son after a terrible motorcycle accident. He had survived, but with severe brain damage. She said the ensuing stress of caring for her adult son cost her friend her marriage, her job, and her own health. "So," she concluded, "you have to be careful what you pray for. I don't pray for healing anymore." Another person in the waiting room spoke up. "God is not a sadist," he said. The young woman asked him to explain what he meant. "God isn't a genie who tries to trick you into wishing for the wrong thing," he said. "God isn't looking for loopholes in a contract when God answers prayer." He went on to paraphrase Romans 8:26: "When we don't know what to pray, the Holy Spirit prays for us with sighs too deep for words." The conversation went on for quite some time, and in the end every-one concluded that the wording of a prayer didn't matter so much as the fact that we pray at all. The incident reminded me that we learn from one another as we reach out with compassion to explain the way of God more accurately to one another.

The teachings of the church about God are sometimes distorted and need to be corrected. For example, some people may think that the saying "God helps those who help themselves" is a line from the Bible. It is actually a line from Ben Franklin's *Poor Richard's Almanac*.[1] Correcting information about Christian faith doesn't mean that the church has all the answers. All it means is that people have been going on faith journeys together for thou-sands of years. It only makes sense to learn from their wisdom.

Integrating Heart, Head, and Life
Colossians 3:12-17

In Colossians 3:12-17, we find an eloquent and practical summary of the early church's understanding of God's way of life through Jesus Christ.

The early church did not talk about Christianity and did not think of what they were doing as a new religion. They referred to what they lived and believed as "the Way." They lived, worked, worshiped, and learned together. They understood that they were on a spiritual journey together and what united them was Jesus. Many people in our society think of Christianity as a set of beliefs with which someone agrees or disagrees. The Scripture illuminates the understanding of the early church that being a follower of Jesus is a way of life and practice according to God's commandment of love. They were a community of learners, disciples who practiced a discipline. Colossians describes the healthy community in which true teaching and learning about Christian life can best occur. The community is called to compassion, kindness, humility, meekness, patience, forgiveness, love, peace, and gratitude. In this atmosphere, the community is called to learn and teach about God. "Let the word of Christ dwell in you richly; teach and admonish one another in all wisdom" (Colossians 3:16).

The Church Teaches a Way of Life

Teaching is more than sharing information. Teaching is about transformation. The church continues to be a community of learners. We are disciples, those who follow Jesus and hope to grow to be like him. We do not teach a set of facts that can be regurgitated on a quiz. We teach a renewed life that can be lived today.

I remember my high school English teacher standing in front of our class holding open a dog-eared copy of *To Kill a Mockingbird* in one hand, his other hand raised in the air, trembling. His voice shook with anger and sadness. His eyes were wet behind his glasses as he read the story and quoted Jem's anguished words to his father after witnessing an innocent African American man receive a guilty verdict at the hands of a white jury: "It ain't right, Atticus! It ain't right." Into those few words he packed all the frustration at all the injustice in the world. As our teacher read them, Jem's passion for justice became his passion and his passion became ours. The church is called to this transforming passion as it teaches God's way of life in Jesus Christ. At its best, the church teaches in a way that shapes us into the image of Christ.

Here's Why I Care

How would your spiritual journey be different if you did not have someone with whom to share questions and answers? How has God used other people to teach you about God? If you were to pass on the wisdom you have learned to another generation, what would you want to teach? What would you want to make sure they learned about God? What would you want to make sure they learned about being human?

A Prayer

God, we thank you for teachers who have taught us by their example as well as their words. We know that when we want to be like them, we are getting a glimpse of the life you want for us. Help us grow intentionally, to learn on purpose, so we may also teach others how to seek you; in Christ we pray. Amen.

---

[1]From *vlib.us/amdocs/texts/prichard36.html.*

Chapter Four

THE CHURCH
Serves

Bible Readings
Micah 6:1-10; Matthew 25:31-46; Luke 10:25-37; Acts 6:1-7;
James 2:14-17; 1 Peter 4:7-11

The Questions
People in churches often use the word *ministry*. *To minister* means "to serve
others." What does it mean to serve? What does the Bible say about how the
church serves?

A Psalm

Happy are those whose help is the God of Jacob,

>whose hope is in the LORD their God,

who made heaven and earth,

>the sea, and all that is in them;

who keeps faith forever;

>who executes justice for the oppressed;

>who gives food to the hungry.

>Psalm 146:5-7

A Prayer

God, we hear your call over the busy-ness of our daily life. Help us find fulfillment in a life of love, of service to one another, and in a growing understanding of your kingdom. Let us be your agents, to help your will be done on earth as it is in heaven. Amen.

Wired to Serve

I'll be honest. For most of my life I've hated the verb *serve*. As a child I sometimes felt as if all I ever heard in church were these irritating concepts: service, giving, self-denial. I associated the idea of serving others with guilt. Service was a burden put upon me by language heavy with "oughts" and "shoulds." Perhaps part of our reluctance to serve comes from the fact that we usually think in terms of scarcity rather than abundance. We feel as if we never have enough time or money for ourselves. How can we have enough to share with others? Yet the Bible teaches that God is the giver of all good things, and we all have more than enough of something.

Recent research has shown that sharing out of our abundance leads to lasting happiness. In one experiment by researchers at the University of British Columbia, research subjects were given money to spend on themselves or on others. Those who spent it on others felt happier at the end of the day.[1] Part of this effect may be that giving money away makes us feel wealthy. However, I believe it is also because we are *wired* to serve others; and the church as the gathered people of God is also wired to serve others.

What Does the Lord Require?
Micah 6:6-8

In Micah 6:6-8, the prophet teaches that worship is deeply connected to service that emerges from kindness, justice, and our relationship with God.

What's in the Bible?
Read Micah 6:6-8. What appeals to you or challenges you in this Scripture? How does it connect to service? How do you think worship, justice, kindness, and walking humbly with God overlap?

In Chapter 2, we explored worship; but worship is just the beginning of a life of faith in God. Micah and other prophets understood this. God requires God's people to "do justice," to "love kindness," and to "walk humbly" with God. Such actions are not only noteworthy, God requires them. Authentic worship moves beyond piety and devotion into a life of service. We do justice and love kindness when we help one another. Love of God and neighbor becomes real as we serve one another.

Yet, ministry is messy. As pastor of outreach for the church I serve, I sometimes have to field calls from needy people who are in crisis. They do not have enough food to eat or enough money to pay their rent or utilities. Sometimes I'm able to refer them to partner agencies that are better equipped to handle their immediate problems—food pantries, utility assistance programs, and so on. Other times we buy groceries, pay rent, or help them out of their immediate crisis; but often, for one reason or another, their deeper problems are not easily fixed.

Some Christians lose patience when discussing these systemic issues because they are much more controversial, political, and complex than stocking a food pantry or giving money to a panhandler. Yet empowering the poor and working with people to change their situation transforms the one serving and the one served. Sometimes we distinguish between relief, which is immediate aid to the poor; development, which is long-term work to empower individuals or a community; and justice, which is addressing unfair political and economic systems. All are legitimate forms of Christian service.

Rather than excusing Christians from compassion, though, these situations should move the church toward doing justice. Justice often involves going beyond handing out money or food to the poor. It means beginning to ask hard questions about why people are poor. Sales taxes on groceries and lack of adequate public transportation make life more difficult for people who are poor. Lack of decent health care keeps people sick and poor. The prophet Isaiah has harsh words for leaders who "write oppressive statutes, / to turn aside the needy from justice / and to rob the poor of my people of their right" (Isaiah 10:1-2). Churches serve as God requires by finding ways to address the causes of poverty as well by providing for immediate needs.

What do you think it means to do justice? What examples come to mind?

R
E
F
L
E
C
T

Being a Neighbor
Luke 10:25-37

The parable of the good Samaritan is one of the most famous Jesus stories of the Bible. It is one that many people live out every time someone stops to help a stranded motorist on the side of the road. This parable challenged the stereotypes and prejudices of Jesus' day and challenged listeners to serve others by *being* a neighbor.

What's in the Bible?
Read Luke 10:25-37. What stands out to you about the story Jesus told? What challenges you in this story? How do you define neighbor?

Jesus' story is a stinging indictment of faith that doesn't express itself in deeds. The first two characters who walked by the wounded man were religious leaders. They turned a blind eye to the dying man. While Jesus did not tell why they walked by the wounded man, it may be that if they had touched him, they would have risked becoming unclean and thus would have been unable to serve in the Temple. Although they believed in God, they did not love their neighbor. The character who "got it," who did what God desired, was not someone from within the religious community but was a Samaritan. I imagine the crowd gasped when Jesus said the word *Samaritan*. Jesus' words would be scandalous because Jews and Samaritans had a history of enmity between them. In answer to the lawyer's question, "Who is my neighbor?" Jesus pointed out that "love your neighbor" is a universal command and encompasses everyone.

Christians are called to develop relationships of mercy, kindness, and justice with human beings in need. Jesus modeled face-to-face compassion. He touched and healed. He traversed social classes to mingle with the poor and rich alike. He lived a life of self-giving, not merely check-writing or protest-marching. In our society it is far too easy to sequester ourselves among people of our own class or ethnicity, to live and work with people just like us. It is far more faithful to the ministry of Jesus Christ to make friends with those who are outside our own social circle and economic class.

When is a time when you were conflicted about helping someone? When service made you uncomfortable? How did you deal with your discomfort? What do you think God teaches us in these situations?

REFLECT

The precedent of including all of humanity under the category of "neighbor" was set long before Jesus told the story of the good Samaritan. There are two love commands in Leviticus, though we often only remember "love your neighbor as yourself" (Leviticus 19:18). Just a few verses later, in Leviticus 19:33-34, God also commands the Israelites to love the foreigner among them as they love themselves. So whether someone is a neighbor or a foreigner, we are to love them as ourselves. There is no distinction. Jesus' answer to the question, "Who is my neighbor?" is "everyone."

Loving our neighbor and loving God go hand-in-hand. A letter from John asserts that "those who love God must love their brothers and sisters also" (1 John 4:21). It is not possible to love God without loving our neighbors, and by loving our neighbors we get a glimpse of the love of God. In Jesus' story, the Samaritan who stopped to help the wounded man on the side of the road actually demonstrated God's love more than the religious professionals who walked on by. He demonstrated the two great commandments in one action of mercy.

Have you ever received helped in a time of need from an unexpected person? Have you ever helped a complete stranger? What were these experiences like for you?

R E F L E C T

Criteria for Judgment
Matthew 25:31-46

Matthew 25:31-46 gives an account of judgment of all the nations at the return of the Son of Man. The criteria for judgment is consistent with all biblical teaching about acting with mercy, kindness, and justice, especially toward those in need.

What's in the Bible?
Read Matthew 25:31-46. What does this reading cause you to feel or think? What challenges you? What do you think Jesus meant when he said, "As you did it to one of the least of these . . . , you did it to me"?

57

The righteous, those who have lived according to God's way, will enjoy eternal life. They have responded to God's word with actions, mercy, and justice by giving food and water to the hungry and thirsty. Attending to such needs imitates the actions of Jesus and makes God's way of life real in a broken and sinful world. In contrast, those who have not acted with mercy and justice toward the hungry and thirsty will be condemned. Faith in God and identity as God's people are proven through actions of mercy, kindness, and justice.

A friend of mine visited Shepherd's Field near Bethlehem a few years ago, the purported site of the angels appearing to the shepherds on that first Christmas. She said that as her tour group paused to read some of the shepherding stories from the Bible, a shepherd with a flock of sheep and goats walked past. The shepherd gave one whistle and a shout, and the flock divided on command—the sheep in one direction and the goats in another.

Though many religious people spend a lot of time trying to figure out who are the sheep and who are the goats, who are the "saved" and who are the "damned," the interesting thing about Jesus' story of the sheep and the goats is that neither group recognized Jesus' close identification with the poor and needy. Both groups were completely surprised. Those who served the poor, sick, and imprisoned did not realize at the time what they were doing. They simply acted out of love. Those who ignored the least probably thought of themselves as good people and most likely believed that they loved Jesus. Yet their actions showed that they did not love their neighbors or show mercy to those who needed it. According to John's letter (1 John 4:20), they did not love God because they did not love their brothers and sisters.

We often read the story of the sheep and the goats as if it's a threat. We hear, "You'd better serve or else" or "you'd better love or else." However, I prefer to interpret this story a different way. If someone goes through their whole life and never learns the joy of serving, if they live their whole life and only associate with those of their own socioeconomic class, if they never become friends with someone who has to struggle just to get by, then they are already experiencing hell. They do not know the joy of serving and loving the least of these, so they do not know the abundant life that Jesus offers. Their life is flat, two-dimensional, and unfulfilling.

Conflict About Serving
Acts 6:1-7

Acts 6:1-7 offers a glimpse of the early church and its practical solution to resolving a conflict about serving.

In Acts 6:1-7, a question exists about whether the issue is about food being distributed to the Hellenist widows or about whether the widows are being discriminated against or neglected in their ministry. The word that is translated "the daily distribution" can also be translated as "ministry" or "service." The Hellenists were Greek-speaking Jews and Jewish Christians; and the Hebrews spoke Greek, Hebrew, and Aramaic. This distinction points to the cultural, ethnic, and linguistic differences that existed among these early Jewish followers of the way of Jesus. The conflict was resolved by dividing tasks of ministry and appointing seven people to attend to the ministry. The story reveals that even in the early church, living as God's people involved working through real differences and finding practical solutions to God's call to serve others.

Many people think that mission work and service is what they pay the church to do; but since we are the church, service is our job. Every member of the body of Christ has a role to play. One preacher friend says, "Ministry requires two physical things: bodies and money. Without those, ministry doesn't happen." Though it often sounds crass to people used to thinking about religion as a private, spiritual matter, the fact is that putting faith into action involves mobilizing our bodies and our resources.

How have conflicts or differences of opinion about serving others been worked through in your church? Who are the people who actually "do" the ministries? How do they serve?

REFLECT

Putting Faith Into Action
James 2:14-18

James 2:14-18 squarely confronts the issue of faith and action, and the message is the same as in other places in the Bible. You can't have one without the other.

What's in the Bible?
Read James 2:14-18. How do you respond to this Scripture? What challenges you or appeals to you? How do you respond to the idea that faith without works is dead?

The entire Book of James elaborates what it means to live as God's people through Jesus Christ. It includes instructions for living together as a church and for serving others. True faith, true relationship with God, is expressed in deeds of mercy and kindness. In James, faith is not separate from attending to the needs of those who suffer or who are poor.

I remember a mission trip in which I questioned the way our faith was being put into action. I rode with my friend Terry in his truck down a narrow tree-lined highway in rural Alabama. We were on our way to a team-training workshop to prepare for our upcoming mission trip to Bolivia. He talked excitedly about our trip and the dormitory we were going to build for a school in the Amazon rainforest. I was a bit more skeptical. I remember saying that although I was looking forward to the experience, I didn't think it made economic sense to go to Bolivia. I said that the money I was spending on airfare, lodging, and meals would probably go a lot further if we simply wrote a check to pay other people to provide the labor in our place. The hired workers in Bolivia would probably be a lot more skilled anyway.

Then we went to Bolivia, and my view completely changed. After our plane landed in La Paz at the highest airport in the world, we attended worship at a small church. The congregation asked me to preach and patiently listened to my halting sermon as an interpreter translated. After I had spoken, people began coming forward to kneel. They asked our team to lay hands on them, and they asked me to pray for them. I felt completely inadequate. Although intellectually I believed in the possibility of miraculous healing, I had never been asked to put that notion into action. One old woman had a pain in her stomach. Another man was going blind. Another young woman prayed for her child. I doubted God, and I doubted myself.

Yet as I knelt down with them and put my hands on their shoulders, I felt the presence of God as real and powerful as a hand on my shoulder. I suddenly knew that it didn't matter the tiniest bit what I felt or whether or not I was up to the task. God had a specific mission for me right there in that place, and that mission was to pray for healing for those people as if our lives depended on it. While we prayed, I remembered what I had been talking about with Terry weeks before; and all my previous hang-ups about the economic effectiveness of foreign mission trips seemed absurd to me. I realized that nothing—no amount of money, good intentions, economic strategy, or feelings of guilt or duty—has as much meaning as an act of human love.

How do you define acts of human love? What are examples? How do they connect to serving others?

REFLECT

Serve One Another
1 Peter 4:7-11

1 Peter 4:7-11 is an inspiring summary of the Christian life of serving one another. It embraces the principles that guide all life together in the community of faith.

What's in the Bible?
Read 1 Peter 4:7-11. How do you respond to this Scripture? What qualities define life together? How do they relate to serving one another?

We often get the idea of service the wrong way around. We talk about service as a Christian obligation, but it is a joy and a privilege. Peter encouraged the church to serve one another with "whatever gift each of you has received." Every human being has God-given talents and skills they can share with others. Some of us are good at teaching, some at managing money, some at financial support, some at encouraging, some at music or poetry. As we saw in Chapter 1, Paul's notion is that each of us has a role, a particular skill or set of talents, that we use as part of the body of Christ. When all those parts are working together in service to the body and to the world, the body is healthy and the work of God gets done. When we serve others with our talents and gifts, we feel talented and gifted. We feel fulfilled when we use the abilities God has given us. We serve one another within and outside the church when we maintain love, when we are hospitable, and when we serve one another with our unique gifts. Perhaps the most reassuring part of this Scripture is that this way of life is empowered by God. "Whoever serves must do so with the strength that God supplies, so that God may be glorified in all things through Jesus Christ" (1 Peter 4:11). According to Jesus, the only way that the world will know Christians is by their love (John 13:34-35)

—not our fish stickers or our doctrine or anything else—our love. Love is the primary defining characteristic of a Jesus-follower. Love defines what service is all about.

Bible Facts
The Greek word that is translated as "serve" in 1 Peter 4:8 is diakoneō. *It also means "minister."*

BIBLE FACTS

The Church and Its Ministry

In the four chapters of this book, we have looked at what the Bible reveals to us about what it means to be the church, God's people gathered together as followers of Jesus Christ. The church and its ministry is all about honoring God and making God's way of life known to others through Jesus Christ. We have seen that the church's life of worship, teaching, and serving blend together into one. Worship overlaps teaching as we proclaim and hear God's story. The church's teaching becomes service as we learn to meet Jesus in the least among us, and our service becomes worship as we give glory to God by loving our neighbors.

Here's Why I Care

The church is called to continue Jesus' ministry on earth. How have you been equipped to serve others? What gifts, talents, or material blessings do you have that could be put to use serving others? How will you live out God's love in your life?

A Prayer

Jesus, you show us the example of true service by becoming one of us, walking and living among us, and serving us. You tell us that the least among us is the greatest and the greatest is the least. You turn the world upside down with your teaching and your ministry. Help us follow your example so that we, too, might turn the world upside down and realize the depth of your amazing love. Amen.

---

[1]From *http://news.bbc.co.uk/2/hi/health/7305395.stm.*

APPENDIX
PRAYING THE BIBLE

Praying the Bible is an ancient process for engaging the Scriptures in order to hear the voice of God. It is also called *lectio divina*, which means "sacred reading." You may wish to use this process in order to become more deeply engaged with the Bible readings offered in each chapter of this study book. Find a quiet place where you will not be interrupted, a place where you can prayerfully read your Bible. Choose a Bible reading from a chapter in this study book. Use the following process to "pray" the Bible reading. After you pray the Bible reading, you may wish to record your experience in writing or through another creative response using art or music.

Be Silent
Open your Bible, and locate the Bible reading you have chosen. After you have found the reading, be still and silently offer all your thoughts, feelings, and hopes to God. Let go of concerns, worries, or agendas. Just *be* for a few minutes.

Read
Read the Bible reading slowly and carefully aloud or silently. Reread it. Be alert to any word, phrase, or image that invites you, intrigues you, confuses you, or makes you want to know more. Wait for this word, phrase, or image to come to you; and try not to rush it.

Reflect
Repeat the word, phrase, or image from the Bible reading to yourself and ruminate over it. Allow this word, phrase, or image to engage your thoughts, feelings, hopes, or memories.

Pray

Pray that God will speak to you through the word, phrase, or image from the Bible reading. Consider how this word, phrase, or image connects with your life and how God is made known to you in it. Listen for God's invitation to you in the Bible reading.

Rest and Listen

Rest silently in the presence of God. Empty your mind. Let your thoughts and feelings move beyond words, phrases, or images. Again, just *be* for a few minutes. Close your time of silent prayer with "Amen," or you may wish to end your silence with a spoken prayer.